Rain, Hail, Sleet & Snow was originally published as a Junior Science Book and dedicated to helping children understand nature and the world around them.

Rain, Hail, Sleet and Snow

By
Nancy Larrick

Illustrated by
Weda Yap

Bristol, Virginia

Dedication contained in the original volume:

The author is grateful to Dr. Ernest J. Christie, Director of the United States Weather Bureau in New York, for assistance in checking the accuracy of this book.

© 2016 Living Library Press. This edition is a reprint of the original text published by Nancy Larrick and illustrated by Weda Yap in 1961 by Garrard Publishing Company, Champaign, Illinois.

ISBN-10: 978-0-692-81047-7

Living Library Press

P.O. Box 16141

Bristol, VA 24201

Forward to 2016 Edition

When searching for a living book on the subject of weather, our friend Nicole Williams of Sabbath Mood Homeschool, could find none better than *Rain, Hail, Sleet & Snow* by Nancy Larrick. At her suggestion, Living Library Press agreed to make this book available to young people again.

At the time of its original publication, meteorologists had been using weather balloons and airplanes to observe and forecast weather patterns, and the use of satellites was just being pioneered. Today, those methods have been replaced by radar imaging, state-of-the-art satellites, and computer generated models to track and predict storms with superior accuracy. And yet, the basic natural phenomena of weather and climate described in this valuable little book remain unchanged. It is our pleasure to renew young readers' acquaintance with the wonders of the natural world through this simple volume.

Contents

Clouds Tell the Story.......3
All Kinds of Clouds..........9
Rain, Rain, Rain 16
A Flash of Lightning
And a Clap of Thunder 26
Tornadoes and Hurricanes 33
Hail, Sleet and Glaze 37
Snow 42
Dew and Frost 48
Water Goes Up and Down 60
Index 60

Clouds Tell the Story

Look at the sky above you. Today it is clear blue. Tiny clouds drift across like feathers on parade. Far across the pond, great white clouds are rolling up. They seem to pile on top of each other to make a boiling mountain above the trees.

Farmers are watching those clouds. Air pilots are watching, too. They know that clouds can bring rain, hail, sleet, or snow.

Weathermen watch the clouds day and night. To them the clouds tell a story. When clouds are heavy and black, they say, "A storm is coming."

Sometimes a cloud will twist like a giant rope on end. That means: "Tornado!" and weathermen send out a warning.

For years men looked at the clouds as ants do—from underneath. No one had seen a cloud from above.

Then the airplane was invented. Men could fly into the clouds. Like birds, they saw fluffy white clouds all around them.

Often they flew over the clouds. As they looked down, they saw a sea of white. Sometimes it looked like a sea of soapsuds. Always floating. Always moving.

Sometimes a hole would break in the clouds. An air pilot could see the rivers and mountains of the earth. Then the hole would close. Once more clouds made a blanket that hid the earth.

Sometimes a hole will break in the clouds.

From the earth we can see only part of a cloud. We don't know how high it is. We don't know how wide it is. Most important, we can't see all the clouds coming toward us.

Balloons carry instruments to report the weather.

From the air we can learn more. So weather stations began sending up airplanes to get reports on the clouds. They sent up balloons, too, to get reports on the clouds.

That was fine in good weather. But in bad weather, airplanes and balloons have trouble. A heavy storm can bring a balloon down.

But weathermen want to know what happens in a heavy storm. They want a report from above the clouds, even in bad weather.

Today they are getting weather reports from outer space. One of the man-made satellites takes pictures 400 miles above the earth. It works like a TV camera taking pictures as it goes around the earth.

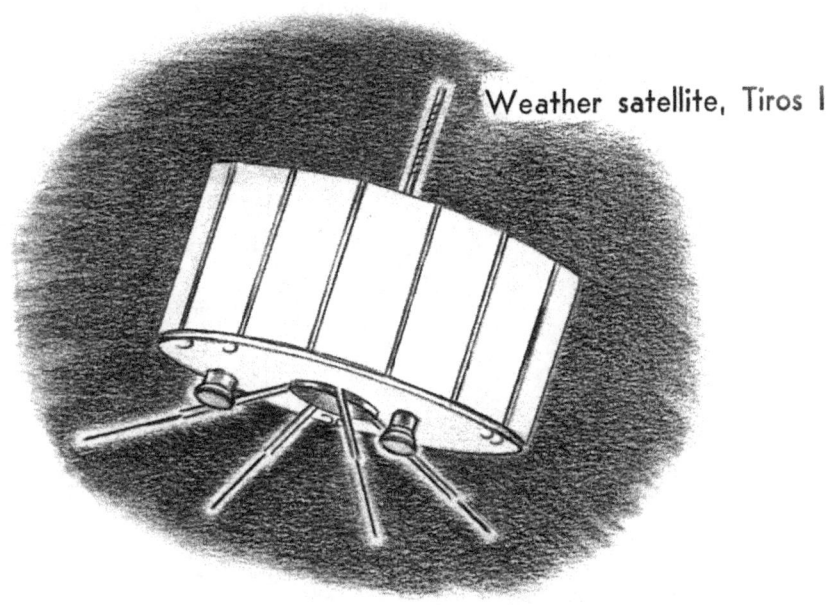

Weather satellite, Tiros I

This man-made satellite sends back pictures of clouds.

Some pictures are 800 miles wide and 800 miles long. One picture shows the clouds from New York to Chicago. Then comes a picture of clouds from Chicago to Denver. In a flash, weathermen see more clouds than they ever saw before.

All Kinds of Clouds

When you breathe out on a cold day, you make a cloud.

When your teapot begins to boil, a cloud appears over the spout.

These are tiny clouds, of course. But they are real clouds.

When you drive into a heavy fog on the road, you are driving into a cloud. It is a cloud resting on the earth.

Sometimes a cloud rests on top of a mountain. If you climb to the top, you are inside the cloud. You can't see the valley below. You can't see the sky above. A cloud is all around you.

Some people call it a fog. And that's what fog is—a cloud resting close to the ground.

Almost every summer morning we see fog over our pond. It seems to rise like a thin cloud of smoke.

This is because the moist air over the pond is warm. At night the land cools more than the water. So the air above it is cool. Warm air from the pond meets cool land air. Moisture turns to the tiniest drops of water. These droplets are so tiny we can hardly imagine what they are like. But they make the air look cloudy.

That is what happens when you breathe out on a cold day. Your breath is warm of course. When it meets the cold air outside, tiny drops of moisture show up. They make a cloud.

Warm moist air from the teapot meets cooler air in your kitchen so the moisture forms little droplets. They make a cloud in the kitchen.

When you look at a cloud in the sky, you are looking at millions and millions of these tiny droplets. For a cloud starts out as moist air. As it cools, moisture begins to form tiny

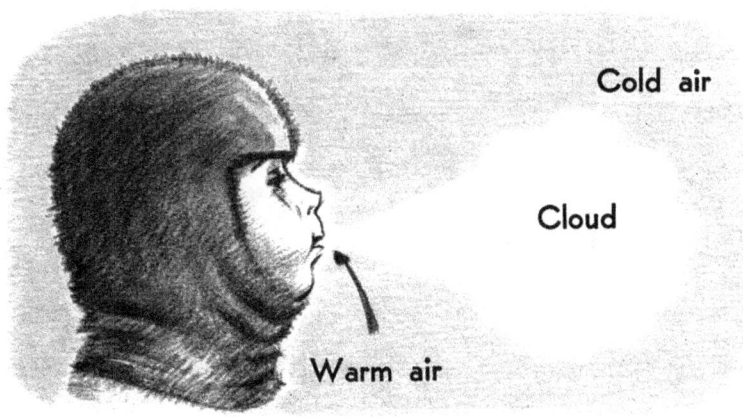

drops. They cling to bits of dust in the air. The cloud rolls up like smoke.

On a clear day, find a big open space and look high in the sky. Do you see some clouds that are like thin streaks or curls?

It seems as though an artist's brush has swept across lightly. A touch here and a touch there. Because these clouds are light and curly, they are called *cirrus* clouds. (*Cirrus* means curl or tuft).

Cirrus clouds are very high in the sky, perhaps four miles or more. It is so cold up

Cirrus clouds

there that cirrus clouds contain tiny ice crystals instead of water droplets.

Often we see cirrus clouds ahead of a storm.

Lower down in the sky, you may see much bigger clouds pushing up. At the top they may look like giant balls of cotton. At the bottom they are flat. All the time they seem to be swelling and boiling up. They may be two or three miles from bottom to top.

These are *cumulus* clouds. On a sunny afternoon, these clouds are likely to be white.

Cumulus clouds

The tops may shine in the sunlight. We might call them "fair weather" clouds.

But sometimes cumulus clouds turn into black storm clouds. Then they reach as high as three or four miles into the sky. Often they bring thunder and lightning as well as rain and hail.

Storm clouds

Stratus clouds

Sometimes the sky seems covered by a gray sheet. You see no blue sky. You see no white clouds. Streaks of gray cover all. It is as though layers of fog had fitted from the earth to the sky.

The gray sheet is really a low cloud. This is called a *stratus* cloud.

As clouds change, the weather is apt to change.

Rain, Rain, Rain

In every cloud there is water. But not every cloud produces rain.

For years men wondered why. Long ago they used magic to try to bring rain. They threw water on each other and roared like thunder. They fired cannons into the air. The Hopi Indians had a snake dance which they hoped would bring rain.

Sometimes rain came. But drumbeating did not bring it. Neither did the rain dancers.

Rain comes from moisture in the clouds themselves. As clouds move, air tosses the tiny droplets of water. If two droplets bump into each other, they make a bigger droplet. With more tossing and bumping, the drops may become bigger and heavier. Then they begin to fall toward the earth. These are raindrops.

In very high clouds, there may be ice crystals as well as water droplets. They, too, are tossed in the air. If they collide, they may stick together and make bigger crystals. When they get big and heavy, they begin to drop. Often they go through a layer of warm air. There they melt. You see them come down as raindrops.

Usually you see the clouds that produce

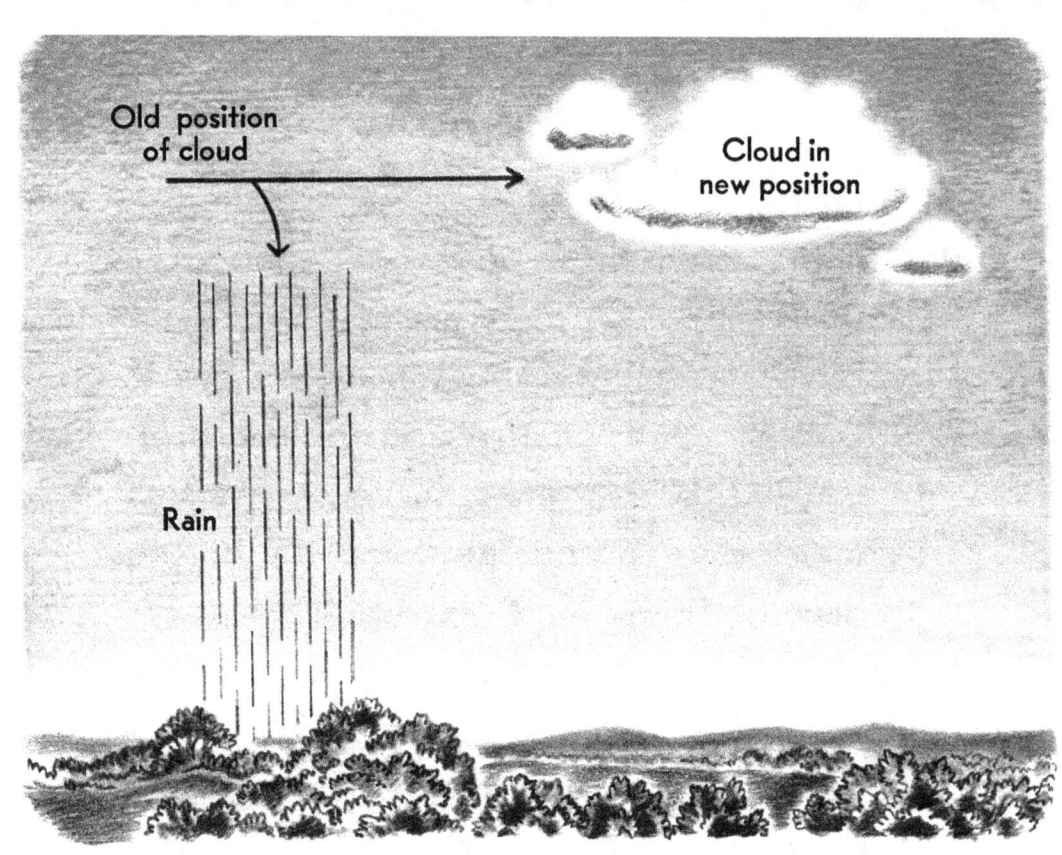

rain. But sometimes you get rain and see no cloud. This may be because the cloud is very high. It may take 20 or 30 minutes for raindrops to fall from such clouds. As they come down, the cloud may be blown away. Then you see raindrops when no cloud is in sight.

Some parts of the world get a great deal of rain. Some get very little.

Scientists measure rainfall with a ruler or yardstick. They find out how deep the rain would be if it could not soak in the ground or run off.

In one year, New York gets 40 inches of rainfall. Chicago gets 30 inches. San Francisco gets about 20 inches.

The driest state is Nevada. It has less than 9 inches of rainfall in a year. The wettest is Louisiana which has about 55 inches.

This tipping bucket measures rainfall.

The heaviest rainfall in the world is in India. One spot in India had over 1,000 inches in a single year.

In one part of Chile, less than one inch fell in 43 years. In a nearby spot, there was no rain at all for 14 years.

Sometimes rain falls faster and harder than at other times. In a moderate rain, only 1/10 to 3/10 of an inch falls in an hour. But one storm in Texas brought 20 inches of rain in three hours. In Pennsylvania, 30 inches fell in five hours. And that rainy spot in India once got 100 inches in just four days.

When a great deal of rain falls in a short time, we sometimes call it a *cloudburst*. Of course, a cloud cannot burst like a bag of water. But when you see so much rain, you can easily think it does.

Why does it rain more in some place

than in others? Why do some clouds produce rain and not others?

First of all, a cloud has to be loaded with moisture to give rain. When air blows over the ocean, it picks up lots of moisture. The clouds become heavy with water droplets.

Often these clouds are blown over the land which is cooler. They are forced up by cool land air. Water droplets in the clouds are whipped by the rising air. Droplets bump into each other and make bigger and bigger

Warm air from the water is forced up by cool land air.

Warm winds from the ocean are laden with moisture.

droplets. As the air rises, rain falls.

On the west coast of India, warm winds sweep in from the Indian Ocean. They are heavy with moisture. When they strike the Himalaya Mountains, they are forced to rise. The tiny water droplets are tossed into each other. As the air rises, heavy rain falls. In one year, 600 inches of rain may fall on the ocean side of the Himalayas. On the other side, there is very little rain. Clouds from the ocean

When it strikes the mountains, the air rises and rain falls.

lose most of their moisture on the ocean side. They never get over the mountains.

Rainfall depends on the amount of moisture in the clouds. It depends, too, on temperature and motion. You see these things working when you blow your warm breath against a cold window glass. Moisture forms on the glass.

There must be something for water to form on. Usually a cloud has millions of dust particles. They are too tiny to see, but moisture clings to them.

But some clouds have little or no dust. Scientists have learned to speed up rain making in such clouds.

They do it by what they call "seeding" the clouds. That is, they spray the clouds with a chemical to which moisture can cling.

Scientific rain makers seed the clouds by plane.

Nowadays, scientific rain makers use silver iodide. Usually they drop it from the wing tips of a plane. Moisture in the cloud clings to the chemical and rain making is under way.

In Texas and Oklahoma, scientific rain makers have been at work in dry seasons. The Australians have experimented too. When the clouds are just right, seeding has brought rain.

But maybe the cloud would have produced rain without the seeding. No one knows. Scientists are trying to find out.

A Flash of Lightning and a Clap of Thunder

It is a hot summer afternoon. The air is quiet and very moist. Fluffy white cumulus clouds begin to form. They pile higher and higher. All the time they are getting darker.

Then a flash of lightning cuts through the dark clouds. Seconds later you hear a clap of thunder.

Strong winds bend the trees to left and right. The air begins to cool. More lightning and thunder. Slowly the wind dies. And rain comes down by the bucketful. It's a thunderstorm all right.

In an hour it may be over. The sun comes out and the air is fresh and brisk. Streets run with water and every leaf is dripping.

But grain in the field may be flat after so much rain. Peach trees may be stripped of their best fruit. The grass is covered by twigs and broken branches broken by the wind.

A huge tree lies across the road—struck by lightning. Or a barn may go up in flames after being hit.

There are almost no thunderstorms near the North and South poles. But in hot climates, thunderstorms strike on about 200 days a year. Sometimes one place will have several thunderstorms in a day.

Usually there are two strong air currents in a thunderstorm. In front, there is a rising current of warm air. Away from it, there is a down current of cool air.

Ice crystals and raindrops form and begin to fall within the cloud. As they scrape past each other, an electrical charge is built up.

The lightning you see is a huge electric spark. It may strike within the cloud or between two clouds. Or it may lead from a cloud to the earth.

Within one storm there may be 1,000 flashes of lightning. And a single lightning stroke may have as many as 30 million volts

When lightning strikes, it usually hits high pointed objects.

of electricity. Each year more than 200 people in the United States are killed by lightning. Thousands of buildings are set on fire by the electric sparks of lightning.

When lightning strikes, it usually hits the high pointed objects. In a city, it generally seeks out the tallest skyscraper. But the steel frame of a building carries the electricity to the ground. And no harm is done. The lightning rod on a house does the same thing.

A lightning rod carries the electricity to the ground.

A TV antenna can act as a lightning rod, too. But it must be properly grounded by a wire leading to the ground.

In a car, the metal body protects passengers from lightning. In a metal airplane, you are pretty safe too.

Outdoors, lone trees attract lightning. So does a person on the beach or in swimming. To escape electricity in the open, it is best to lie flat in a hollow away from a lone tree.

After a flash of lightning, you hear a clap of thunder. What is that? Long ago people said it meant that gods were angry.

Now we know that a sudden flash of lightning heats the air so greatly that it causes a giant crash. Lightning and thunder happen in the same split second.

But light travels almost a million times faster than sound. So you see the flash of lightning. And later you hear the clap of thunder.

Often a thunderstorm comes and goes quickly. Sometimes the clouds will break while it is still raining.

Then the sun comes out. And if everything is just right, you may see a rainbow. Across the sky there is a misty arch of color. Red, orange, yellow, green, blue, purple, and violet fade into each other.

Sunlight and raindrops make the rainbow. Each raindrop acts like a tiny prism. As the sun strikes many raindrops, the light is broken into many rainbow colors.

One time I saw two rainbows at once. One arch above the other. They made a great double-decker bridge I shall never forget.

Tornadoes and Hurricanes

A tornado is the most violent kind of storm. It begins with large clouds and rumbling thunder. Then a black cloud stretches into a long thin column. It looks like a rope twisting towards the ground. The wind at the center may blow at 200 or 300 miles an hour.

In the middle, the whirling air rushes upward. Heavy rain and hail come down. Lightning flashes. There is a strange hissing sound as the air rushes up the center.

Roofs are torn off. Porches are swept away. Heavy objects are lifted by the rising column of air and carried for hundreds of feet. Even houses and cars have been sucked up by the twisting air.

Tightly closed buildings sometimes explode in the storm.

Yet a tornado is a small storm, and it passes quickly. Generally it is no more than a quarter of a mile wide. It moves at about 30 miles an hour. So in less than a minute, a tornado can strike in one spot, do its damage, and move on.

A hurricane is a much bigger storm. It may be as much as 200 miles across. It moves slowly, but the winds within a hurricane may whirl at 150 to 200 miles an hour.

A hurricane begins over the ocean. The air is moist and hot. Winds coming from different directions begin to whirl about each other. Air in the middle rises faster and faster. Moisture accumulates.

As the storm sweeps over the land, wind and rain pour forth. High winds lash the trees and rip off chimneys and rooftops.

The eye of a hurricane

Heavy rains cause streams and rivers to overflow. Floods destroy homes and sweep away cattle.

A tornado may be over in half a minute. A hurricane may last two to four hours in any one place.

A barometer is used to forecast the weather.

Hail, Sleet, and Glaze

Some hot afternoon watch a thunderstorm closely. You will see a heavy downpour of rain. And if everything is just right, you may see hailstones coming down. They look like marbles made of ice.

Often hailstones are as big as mothballs. Sometimes they are as big as baseballs. One hailstone in Nebraska weighed a pound and a half and was 17 inches around.

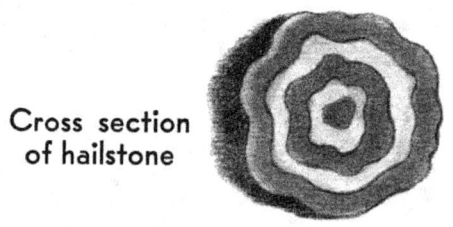

Cross section of hailstone

If you could cut a hailstone in half, you would see many layers of ice. They look like the layers of an onion.

A hailstone begins as a raindrop in a thundercloud. It freezes in the upper cloud. As it starts to fall, an air current lifts it again. It may make several up-and-down trips. Each time it may pick up more moisture. And it may add another layer of ice.

It is fun to see hailstones bounce as they hit the sidewalk. But it's no fun for the farmer when hail hits his crops.

Hailstones rise and fall within a cloud.

Apples are covered with holes and knocked to the ground. Wheat is beaten down. Tobacco leaves are cut to shreds.

In a hailstorm, windows are often smashed. Automobiles are badly dented. Horses and cows suffer broken bones. In 1932, 200 people were killed by hailstones in China.

Sleet is smaller than hail. It usually comes in cold weather. But like hail it begins as rain. As a raindrop falls through the cloud, it may touch a cold layer of air and freeze. It falls as a clear bead of ice.

Sleet does not bounce up and down in a cloud like hail. But it can hit the ground hard enough to bounce.

Both hail and sleet are frozen *before* they strike the earth.

Sometimes rain freezes *after* it falls to the ground. This happens when very cold rain strikes cold surfaces. Then the rain forms a glaze of ice on everything it touches. As more rain falls, the glaze grows thicker.

After an ice storm, every twig is covered

with glaze. Electric wires are coated. The fence becomes a pattern of ice.

Sometimes the glaze is so heavy that branches break. Telephone wires sag. Poles lean across the road. Trees bend their tops toward the ground and cars skid on the glaze.

Snow

The next time it snows, try this experiment. Spread out a dark wool scarf to catch a few snowflakes. Or use a dark sweater or skirt.

Then look at the snowflakes through a magnifying glass. They will look much bigger. Every flake is like a lacy star.

Sometimes two or three flakes stick together. Some are broken in falling.

With the glass you see that each perfect snowflake has six sides or six points. But no two are exactly alike. One has six slim arms or rays. The next has six points that look like fern leaves.

When a snowflake touches your warm hand, it melts. But snowflakes are not frozen raindrops like hail and sleet. Instead, they are made from water vapor.

You have seen water in two different forms. One is the liquid you drink. It comes down as rain. Or it may run through the woods in a stream.

Ice is water in its solid form. Hail and sleet are frozen water. Icicles are frozen water. So is glaze.

But sometimes water is invisible. It floats in the air. It is so fine you cannot see it at all. It is called *water vapor*.

Water vapor in the upper air may be so cold that it freezes. It turns to tiny crystals of ice. Or the tiny droplets of water in a cloud may freeze and turn to ice crystals.

These ice crystals are snowflakes. They may grow as they fall through the moist air. If they strike a warm layer, they may melt and fall as raindrops.

Sometimes snowflakes seem to come down in handfuls. Probably these are clumps of snowflakes that stick together. One clump may be 2 inches across.

A single snowflake is probably no larger than 1/2 inch across. And this is unusually large. Generally it would take 16 to 32 snowflakes to make a line one inch long. Some snowflakes are much smaller. It might take 200 of these smallest ones to make a line an inch long.

Snowflakes are fluffy and irregular. As they pile up air pockets form between the starry points and arms. If you could melt 10

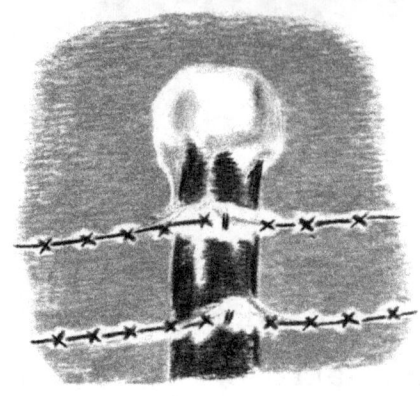

inches of snow, you would have only one inch of water. The rest is air.

Air makes a blanket of snow very white. Because of this, some animals can bury themselves in snow and sleep all winter.

Some snowflakes have sharper points than others. This makes them cling to each other.

On a twig no bigger than a pencil, these snowflakes pile 2 or 3 inches high. On top of a fencepost, you may see 5 or 6 inches of snowflakes. Even electric wires can hold a three inch layer.

On the ground, 4 or even 14 inches of snow does no harm. But a slender twig can break under 3 or 4 inches of snow. Branches are weighed down and broken. And electric wires break under the weight of snow.

You can protect evergreen trees and shrubs in a heavy snowstorm. Shake the snow from their branches before it gets too heavy.

Dew and Frost

Walk through the grass early on a summer morning. Probably your shoes will get wet because the grass and leaves are wet.

Yesterday afternoon the grass was dry. There was no rain during the night.

The water you see is dew. It clings to every blade of grass. It sparkles in the cobwebs.

Dew does not fall like rain. Instead it forms right where you see it. Dew is water vapor that has turned to beads of water.

In the summer the air is often heavy with water vapor. At night the earth cools quickly. Leaves and grass cool, too.

When water vapor touches them, it grows cool, also. As it cools, it turns to tiny beads of water. This is *dew*.

Probably you have seen dew form on a glass of ice water, too. The glass is dry when you fill it with ice. Then tiny beads of water appear on the outside. The water does not come from inside the glass, it comes from water vapor in the air outside.

Ice makes the glass cold. When moist air touches the cold glass, the water vapor cools. Cooled water vapor turns to water and forms tiny beads of water on the outside of the glass.

Dew

If you wear glasses, you have seen them covered with a mist of water. It happens when you come from the cold out of doors into a warm room. The warm, moist air indoors strikes the cold glasses. Water vapor in the air is cooled. It forms tiny beads of water on the cool glasses. This is dew from water vapor indoors.

Sometimes cool air outdoors makes the glass in your window cool, too. The air indoors may be warm and moist. When it touches the cool glass, water vapor turns to water. You see a film of dew on the inside of the window.

In very cold weather, the water vapor freezes as it touches the cold glass.

Frost on window glass

You see tiny ice crystals, or frost. Often they make a lacy pattern on the window. This is not frozen dew. The water vapor has turned directly to frost. This can happen when the temperature is 32 degrees or less.

On a cold winter morning, frost may form on the ground instead of dew. Every blade of grass seems to be covered with ice crystals.

This happens when the ground and plants are very cold. As water vapor in the air touches them, it freezes. The ground and plants are covered with sparkling frost.

If there is a strong wind, dew and frost are not likely to form. This is because the air keeps moving. So it is not likely to be cooled by the earth. Water vapor is not so likely to turn to dew or frost.

When there are clouds, heat cannot leave the earth so fast. The water vapor is not cold enough to produce dew or frost.

You are most likely to see dew or frost in the early morning. They disappear when the sun warms the air.

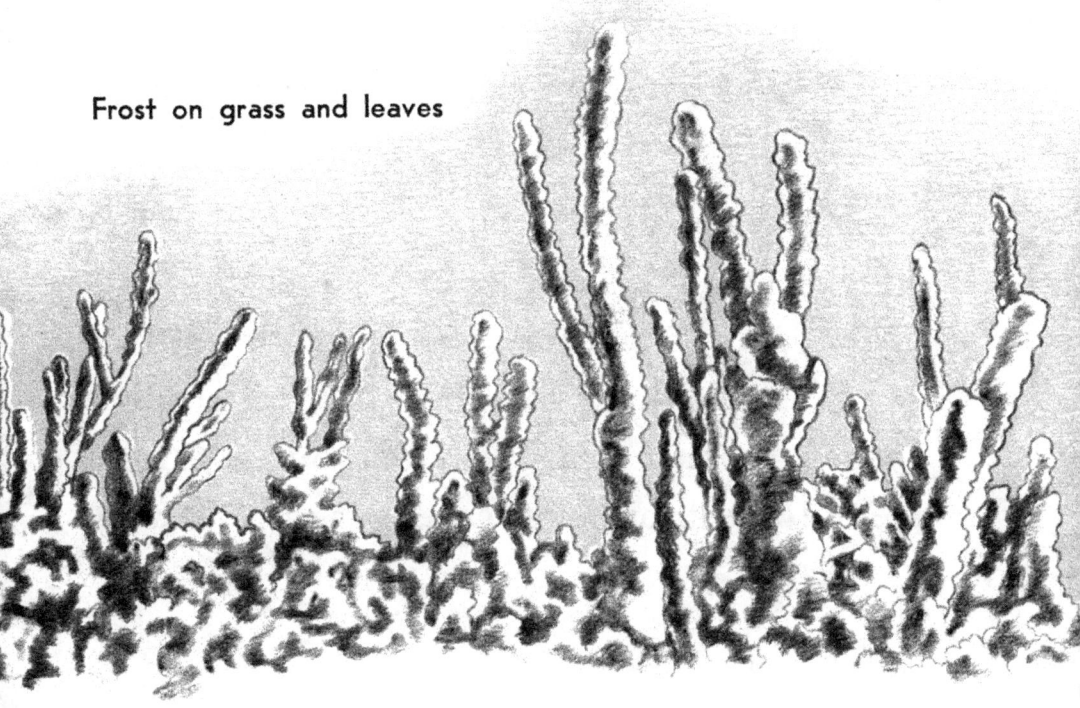

Frost on grass and leaves

Water Goes Up and Down

It is easy to see rain coming down. Or snow. Or hail or sleet. No one can doubt that water comes down from the air to the earth.

It is not so easy to realize that water also goes up from the earth. In fact, ancient people did not know that water goes up as well as down.

When you hang up a wet bathing suit, you know the water will disappear. If the air is dry and hot, the water disappears quickly. Suppose the air is cool and moist. Then it takes longer for the bathing suit to dry

What happens? Water in the bathing suit changes to water vapor which moves into the air. We say the water *evaporates*. You cannot see evaporation because you cannot see water vapor.

On a sunny day the air is often hot and dry. If so, it can take up water more easily.

If the wind is blowing, too, more air touches the wet surface. So evaporation is speeded up.

On a cool cloudy day, the air is likely to be very moist. It may be loaded with water vapor. If so, it cannot take up more water vapor. On that kind of day, evaporation is very slow.

In hot sunshine, water evaporates quickly.

Evaporation is probably going on all around you. Water evaporates from a puddle in the road. It evaporates from the surface of ponds, lakes, and rivers. It evaporates from the ocean. Water even evaporates from plants.

On a warm summer day, a sunflower gives off a pint of water in the form of water vapor. A big oak tree may give off as much as 200 gallons of water in a day.

There is always water in the air. Sometimes the air reaches the point it can hold no more water. This is called the *saturation* point or the *dew point.*

The amount of water in the air is called the *humidity.* This is always changing.

Weather reports tell of *relative humidity.* This means the amount of water in the air in relation to the temperature.

Warm air can hold more water than cold air. When warm moist air is cooled, it loses some of its water vapor. Perhaps the water vapor will become tiny droplets in a cloud. Or it may become rain and fall to the earth. Or it may become dew on the grass.

When water vapor changes to water, we say it *condenses.* Water vapor condenses when it touches the cool grass. Then we have dew.

When the dew disappears in the warm sun we say it *evaporates*. It has changed to water vapor which we cannot see.

All the time, water is going up and down. From the pond it *evaporates*—goes into the air as water vapor. But later it will *condense* and come down again—perhaps as rain, hail, sleet, or snow.

From the earth the water rises as water vapor.
It comes down again as rain, hail, sleet or snow.

Index

Air, 10, 11, 17, 22, 52-53, 54-55, 58
Air Currents, 28, 38
Air Pilots, 3, 4
Airplane, 4, 6, 25

Barometer, 36
Blanket of Clouds, 5
Breath, 11, 23

Cannons, 16
Cirrus Clouds, 12, 13
Clouds, 3, 4, 5, 6, 7, 8, 9-15, 16-18, 20-21, 23-25, 26-28, 31, 33-38, 40, 44, 55
   TV pictures of, 8
Cloudburst, 20
Condensation, 57-58
Cumulus Clouds, 13-14, 26

Dew, 48-53, 58
Dewpoint, 57
Droplets of water, 10, 11, 17, 20, 21, 22, 44, 57
Dust, 12, 23-24

Earth, 4, 7, 9, 14, 52, 54
Electricity, 28-29, 31
Evaporation, 55-58

Farmers, 3, 38
Fog, 9, 10, 15
Frost, 52-53

Glaze, 40-41

Hail, 3, 14, 34, 37-40, 43, 44, 54, 58
Hailstones, 37-38, 40
Hailstorm, 39-40

Himalaya Mountains, 22-23
Hopi Indians, 16
Humidity, 57
Hurricane, 33-36

Ice, 44, 49
Ice crystals, 12-13, 17, 28, 44, 52
Ice storm, 40-41
Icicles, 44

Land, 21
Light, speed of, 31
Lightning, 14, 26-31, 34
Lightning rods, 30

Magic, 16
Moisture, 10, 11, 12, 17, 21, 22, 35
Mountains, 10, 22-23

Ocean, 21, 35, 56

Pond, 10, 56
Prism, 32

Rain, 3, 14, 16-25, 49, 54, 58
Rain dancers, 17
Rain makers, 24-25

Rainbow, 32
Raindrops, 17, 18, 28, 38, 40, 43, 44
Rainfall, 19-20
Relative humidity, 57

Saturation point, 57
Scientists, 24-25
Seeding clouds, 24-25
Silver iodide, 24
Sky, 3, 10, 11, 14, 15
Skyscraper, 29
Sleet, 3, 40, 43, 44, 54, 58
Snake dance, 16
Snowflakes, 42-46
Sound, speed of, 31
Storm, 4, 6, 13, 20, 28, 33-36
Stratus clouds, 14
Sun, 27, 31, 32

Temperature, 23, 52, 57
Thunder, 14, 26-31, 33
Thunderstorm, 27, 28, 31, 37, 38
Tiros I, 7
Tornado, 4, 33-36
TV antenna, 30
TV camera, 7

61

Water, 16, 23, 44, 48-52, 54-58
Weather, 6, 7, 15
Weather balloons, 6, 7
Weather reports, 7
Weather statellite, 7
Weather stations, 6
Weathermen, 4, 7
Wind, 27, 33-35, 52, 55

www.ingramcontent.com/pod-product-compliance
Lightning Source LLC
Chambersburg PA
CBHW072107290426
44110CB00014B/1862